Henry VI, Part I

David Oyelowo trai... ... Dramatic Arts. In his relatively short yet distinguished career, David has garnered honours for his work in theatre, film, television and radio. His first professional appearance on the London stage was in *The Suppliants* at The Gate theatre, for which he received an Ian Charleson award nomination. For the RSC he appeared alongside Alan Bates and Frances Delatour in *Antony and Cleopatra*, *Volpone*, and an adaptation of Aphra Behn's *Oroonoko*. He went on to be the first black actor to play an English King for the RSC as Henry VI in the company's formidable eight play staging of 'The Histories'. His critically acclaimed portrayal of the Christian King won him an *Evening Standard* Best Newcomer Award nomination and the Ian Charleson Award for Best Newcomer in a Classical Role.

David has both British and Hollywood film credits and is one of the leads in the acclaimed BBC spy drama, *Spooks*.

Colin Nicholson is the originator and editor for the *Actors on Shakespeare* series published by Faber and Faber.

in the same series

A Midsummer Night's Dream / F. MURRAY ABRAHAM
Henry IV, Part I / SIMON CALLOW
Henry IV, Part II / SIMON CALLOW
Twelfth Night / EMMA FIELDING
Othello / JAMES EARL JONES
Julius Caesar / CORIN REDGRAVE
Antony and Cleopatra / VANESSA REDGRAVE
Much Ado About Nothing / SASKIA REEVES
Richard II / FIONA SHAW
Macbeth / HARRIET WALTER
King Lear / NICOL WILLIAMSON

DAVID OYELOWO

Henry VI, Part I

Series Editor: Colin Nicholson

faber and faber

First published in 2003
by Faber and Faber Limited
3 Queen Square London WC1N 3AU

Typeset by Faber and Faber in Minion
Printed in England by Mackays of Chatham, plc

The right of David Oyelowo to be identified as author of this work has
been asserted in accordance with Section 77 of the Copyright, Designs
and Patents Act 1988

The right of Colin Nicholson to be identified as author of the introduc-
tion has been asserted in accordance with Section 77 of the Copyright,
Designs and Patents Act 1988

A CIP record for this book
is available from the British Library

ISBN 0-571-21657-9

10 9 8 7 6 5 4 3 2 1

Introduction

Shakespeare: Playwright, Actor and Actors' Playwright

It is important to remember that William Shakespeare was an actor, and his understanding of the demands and rewards of acting helped him as a playwright to create roles of such richness and depth that actors in succeeding generations – even those with no reason or desire to call themselves 'classical' actors – have sought opportunities to perform them.

As the company dramatist, Shakespeare was writing under the pressure of producing scripts for almost immediate performance by his fellow players – the Lord Chamberlain's Men (later the King's Men), who, as a share-holding group, had a vested interest in their playhouse. Shakespeare was writing for a familiar set of actors: creating roles for particular players to interpret; and, being involved in a commercial enterprise, he was sensitive to the direct contact between player and audience and its power to bring in paying customers. His answer to the challenge produced a theatrical transformation: Shakespeare peopled the stage with highly credible personalities, men and women who were capable of change, and recognizable as participants in the human condition which their audience also shared. He connected two new and important elements: the idea of genuine individuality – the solitary, reflecting, self-communing soul, which is acutely aware of its own sufferings and desires; and, correlatively, the idea of inner life as something that not only exists but can also be explored. For him, the connection became the motor of dramatic action on the stage, as it is the motor of personal action in real life.

The primary importance of the actor cannot be disputed: it is his or her obligation – assisted to a greater or lesser extent by a director's overall vision of the play – to understand the personality they are representing onstage and the nature of the frictions taking place when that personality interacts with other characters in the drama: Shakespeare's achievement goes far beyond the creation of memorable characters (Macbeth, Falstaff) to embrace the exposition of great relationships (Macbeth–Lady Macbeth; Falstaff–Prince Hal). Great roles require great actors, and there is no group of people in a better position to interpret those roles to *us* than the principal actors of *our* generation – inhabitants of a bloodline whose vigour resonates from the sixteenth century to the present day – who have immersed themselves in the details of Shakespeare's creations and have been party to their development through rehearsal and performance.

Watching Shakespeare can be an intimidating experience, especially for those who are not well versed in the text, or in the conventions of the Elizabethan stage. Many excellent books have been written for the academic market but our aim in this series is somewhat different. *Actors on Shakespeare* asks contemporary performers to choose a play of particular interest to them, push back any formal boundaries that may obstruct channels of free communication and give the modern audience a fresh, personal view. Naturally the focus for each performer is different – and these diverse volumes are anything but uniform in their approach to the task – but their common intention is, primarily, to look again at plays that some audiences may know well and others not at all, as well as providing an insight into the making of a performance.

Each volume works in its own right, without assuming an in-depth knowledge of the play, and uses substantial quotation to contextualize the principal points. The fresh approach of the many and varied writers will, we hope, enhance your enjoyment of Shakespeare's work.

Colin Nicholson
February 2002

Note: For reference, the text used here is
the Arden Shakespeare.

Characters

King Henry the Sixth
Duke of Gloucester, *Uncle to the King, and Protector*
Duke of Bedford, *Uncle to the King, and Regent of France*
Duke of Exeter, *Great-uncle to the King*
Bishop of Winchester, *Great-uncle to the King, and afterwards Cardinal*
Duke of Somerset
Richard Plantagenet, *afterwards Duke of York*
Earl of Warwick
Earl of Salisbury
Earl of Suffolk
Lord Talbot, *afterwards Earl of Shrewsbury*
John Talbot, *his Son*
Edmund Mortimer, *Earl of March*
Sir John Falstaff
Sir William Lucy
Sir William Glansdale
Sir Thomas Gargrave
Mayor of London
Woodville, *Lieutenant of the Tower*
Vernon, *of the White-Rose or York Faction*
Basset, *of the Red-Rose or Lancaster Faction*
A Lawyer. Mortimer's Keepers
A Papal Legate, and two Ambassadors
Charles, *Dauphin, and afterwards King of France*
Reignier, *Duke of Anjou, and titular King of Naples*
Duke of Burgundy
Duke of Alençon

Governor of Paris
Master-Gunner of Orleans, and his son
General of the French Forces in Bordeaux
A French Sergeant. A Porter
An old Shepherd, Father to Joan la Pucelle

Margaret, *Daughter to Reignier, afterwards married to King*
    Henry
Countess of Auvergne
Joan la Pucelle, *commonly called Joan of Aire*

Lords, Warders of the Tower, Heralds, Officers, Soldiers,
    Messengers, and Attendants
Fiends appearing to Joan la Pucelle

Henry VI, Part I (with *Parts II* and *III*) was performed by the Royal Shakespeare Company at the Swan theatre, Stratford-upon-Avon, in November 2000, with the following cast:

Henry VI	David Oyelowo
Humphrey, Duke of Gloucester	Richard Cordery
Duke of Bedford	David Beames
Duke of Exeter	John Kane
Henry Beaufort	Christopher Ettridge
Duke of Somerset	Nicholas Asbury
Richard Plantagenet	Clive Wood
Edmund Mortimer	Jerome Willis
Vernon	Geoffrey Streatfield
Earl of Warwick	Geff Francis
Earl of Suffolk	Richard Dillane
Sir William Lucy	James Tucker
Lord Talbot	Keith Bartlett
John Talbot	Sam Troughton
Alexander Eden	Owen Oakeshott
Sir Thomas Gargrave	Robert Barton
Mayor's Officer	Gavin Marshall
Charles, the Dauphin	Aidan McArdle
Reignier	Rhashan Stone
Duke of Alencon	Tom Beard
Bastard of Orleans	Jake Nightingale
Duke of Burgundy	Philip Brook
Joan la Pucelle	Fiona Bell

Fiends appearing to La Pucelle	Sarah D'Arcy
(Countess of Auvergne)	Aislin McGuckin
The Keeper	Edward Clayton
Keeper's assistant	Neil Madden

Dedicated to Nicholas Hytner
For helping make my dream of becoming an actor a reality.

Foreword

Established now as *Henry VI, Parts I, II* and *III*, when first performed the three plays were variously titled, *Harry the VI*; *The First Part of the Contention of the Two Famous Houses of York and Lancaster*; and *The True Tragedy of Richard Duke of York, with the Death of Good King Henry the Sixth, with the Whole Contention between the Two Houses Lancaster and York*.

Henry VI is the beginning of Shakespeare's own understanding of a world that he described through theatre – the dramatic succession of English history, and *Part I* needs to be considered as the beginning of a cycle, an equal part. *Henry VI* needs to be staged in its entirety, unlike *Henry IV*, where the plays can be viewed separately, or regarded independently. The demands of theatre and performance impose practical restrictions, especially of length and time, and inevitably cuts and edits repackage the History Plays (in general) and *Henry VI* (in particular); *The Misery of Civil War*, *The Roses*, *An Age of Kings*, *The Wars of the Roses*, *The Plantagenets* and *Rose Rage* are some examples.

David Oyelowo's *Henry VI, Part I* clearly shows a young actor rising to the challenge of his first major Shakespeare role, communicating a parallel with the boy king coming to terms with the responsibilities thrust upon him.

Prelude: From Egypt to Rome and Back Again

My journey towards Henry VI began with the little known part of Decretas in *Antony and Cleopatra*. I was on a train to the Barbican to play Dercetas for the Royal Shakespeare Company when my 'phone rang: my agent said the RSC wanted to meet me for *Henry VI, Parts I, II* and *III*; but a bad signal meant I couldn't establish which role and rang off. Later, backstage at the Barbican moments before going onstage, I saw the casting director and asked her which role in *Henry VI*? 'Henry VI'. Yes, I said. 'Henry VI,' she repeated. Yes, but which role? 'Henry VI!'

The following week I met the director, Michael Boyd, for my audition. I couldn't help thinking there had been some kind of mistake; I had only recently graduated from drama school and here I was auditioning for the title role in three plays at the RSC. It was the most nervous I have ever been. What followed was two hours of Michael getting me to do the Molehill speech from *Henry VI, Part III*, over and over and over again. I left the audition feeling despondent; I'd given my best, but thought the audition had lasted two hours because I hadn't managed to give Michael what he was looking for. Several painfully long days later, again on my way to *Antony and Cleopatra*, I received a call from my agent: 'Hello, David, or should I say "my liege"?' I vividly remember that night's performance – watching Alan Bates giving his Antony and Frances DeLatour giving her Cleopatra – thinking, *That's going to be me*. It filled me with both excitement and trepidation.

I had not enjoyed my time on *Antony and Cleopatra*, mainly because I had meatier parts in two other plays at the RSC

1

that season; but it wasn't just that. *Antony and Cleopatra* is a very difficult Shakespeare play to get right. Its copious amount of scenes can be problematic (especially keeping a steadfast hold on the political thread that entwines the love story), with the constant flitting from Egypt to Rome and back again. Trying to separate the political and romantic elements can be a challenge for both the director and the audience. I felt we never really conquered these challenges, and it sometimes felt as if the design, costumes and music were being used to paper over the cracks, which only highlighted the production's failure to clearly communicate the story to the audience.

Another aspect that didn't help this production was the rehearsal period. *Antony and Cleopatra*, by its very nature as an ill-fated love story, is often perceived as a star vehicle. As a result, a lot of time in rehearsal is inevitably spent on the lovers. Unfortunately for us, this was at the expense of the rest of the cast and we were given minimal aid in creating three-dimensional characters, regardless of the size of the part. The supporting players became disillusioned with their roles and functions within the play. This led to a lack of commitment and sympathy with the director's vision, which meant that only the lead players tended to commit fully to any given performance. Alan and Frances soldiered on despite all this and mediocre reviews, which compounded the situation. I couldn't help but wonder how I would have coped under similar circumstances, being comparatively young (I was twenty-four at the time) and inexperienced.

Being in that production made me realize how demanding playing one of Shakespeare's title roles can be, both physically and mentally. Watching seasoned actors call on everything they had in order to conquer the language really did make me wonder whether I was ready to play such a role in not one but three of Shakespeare's plays.

Looking out at the audience that night, feeling as if I was about to get found out, I couldn't help thinking of those people who had encouraged me to pursue acting as a profession suddenly being confronted by their misjudgement. My fears stemmed from the fact that I had always regarded Shakespeare as the dividing line between good actors and great actors. Even after training, there are no qualifications that distinguish a good actor; the only measure you have of your ability is the opinion of others. I knew that, having got this part, I couldn't escape other people's opinions.

In my very short career I had done some Shakespeare, but not a lot. I had played Puck in *A Midsummer Night's Dream* and Aufidius in *Coriolanus* at the Edinburgh Festival, both while I was still at the London Academy of Music and Dramatic Arts (LAMDA); and now I was giving my seven lines as Dercetas in *Antony and Cleopatra*. I had hoped to play great parts in wonderful theatres, but I hadn't dared dream it would happen only two years after drama school.

I had always been aware of the black actors who had essentially opened the doors I was now about to walk through – actors such as Edric O'Connor, the first black actor to appear at the RSC, in 1958; Paul Robeson, who played Othello at the RSC in 1959 (and in the London production of 1930 with Peggy Ashcroft); Rudolph Walker; Hugh Quarshie; in more recent years, actors such as Adrian Lester, Lenny James, David Harewood, and many more. Having admired these actors and their achievements for so long, I was surprised to find that my acquisition of the part would mark the first time a black actor had played an English king at the RSC. Very soon 'pioneer' was being used in relation to my name. It was a nice compliment, but one that caused me to feel weighed down with responsibility. For any minority group struggling for equality, there is an inevitable pressure that comes with being afforded the opportunities it's been fighting for. I felt that, having been awarded this part, I had to be excellent; otherwise I'd give a ready excuse for similar opportunities not to be available to other black actors.

More terrifying than the label 'pioneer' was the sheer amount of baggage that goes with playing any of Shakespeare's major roles: the great actors who have inevitably given 'definitive' performances as Henry VI – Alan Howard and Ralph Fiennes, to name but two – and the fact that there are so many schools of thought on how Shakespeare should be acted and spoken. Having lived in Nigeria during the formative years of my education, in a culture where Shakespeare was less prominent, I had little or no reverence for it, which in the long run proved to be an asset; but it also left me with the misguided notion that I had somehow missed out on receiving the key within the British education system that enables you to unlock Shakespeare.

My parents moved me and my two brothers back to our country of origin in 1982; I was only six years old at the time and we didn't return to England until I was about fourteen. On returning to England I formed the opinion, like a lot of young students, that Shakespeare was boring, unreadable and irrelevant to modern life. It took seeing Robert Lepage's production of *A Midsummer Night's Dream* at the National Theatre in 1992 to open my eyes to the fact that, much like a music score, Shakespeare was primarily written for performance and not solitary reading. I was amazed at the sheer pace of the production: it was fast, visually exciting, funny, and I can honestly say that I understood the play, not just that I loved the story. Up until seeing that production I had felt intellectually incapable of unlocking Shakespeare. Seeing that production was one of the reasons I became an actor.

While at LAMDA, training and watching several Shakespeare productions, I developed theories on how Shakespeare should be played. For instance, I noticed how easily I fell into the trap of being so seduced by Shakespeare's verse that my delivery became a mush of declaimed poetry and demonstrated emotion, rather than living, relevant and immediate drama. I realized that Shakespeare is best performed fast, with clear delivery that doesn't patronize the audience by carefully spelling out what the actor is trying to convey. Knowing that I harboured these theories based more upon watching Shakespeare than on doing it unnerved me, because I now had to put my theories into practice. As it turned out, I didn't have much time to do a lot of worrying: I completed the season playing Dercetas in May and started a film in June, which didn't finish shooting till the day before rehearsals for *Henry*.

Excitement and Trepidation

If there was one thing I was not looking forward to, it was the first read-through. First read-throughs are funny things. They are so nerve-racking because you feel a need to justify to the other actors why you've been given the part, and you don't want the director to feel as if they've made a mistake. This feeling was enhanced for me because I had just spent two months playing a streetwise London DJ with a 'rude boy' West London accent, which I was finding hard to shake off. Even though I had done some research, I felt it was nowhere near enough, considering that the plays covered sixty years of English history. Yet again that fear of being 'found out' rose up in me. It also didn't help that one of the first conversations I had with a member of the cast was with an actor who proceeded to tell me that he had first been with the RSC in 1954 and had subsequently been onstage with both Gielgud and Olivier. Luckily we didn't do a read-through on the first day; I felt I had avoided being exposed, at least for one more day.

As it happened, I didn't get to step into Henry's shoes for another week, because Henry doesn't appear in *Henry VI, Part I* until the third act. It was an absolute gift from God to be afforded a couple of days to get to know everyone, see them work and soak up Michael Boyd's vision for the plays, before having to utter a single line. In this same week I was also fortunate enough to witness one of the most inspiring productions of Shakespeare I had ever seen. It was a production of *Hamlet* at the Globe Theatre in London with Mark Rylance playing Hamlet. The Globe is a theatre built in the style of the Elizabethan theatres of Shakespeare's day and to be perfectly honest I wasn't particularly excited to be going there; I had always thought of the Globe as more of a tourist trap than a real theatre with 'serious' productions. To make matters worse, it was standing room only for one of Shakespeare's longest plays; but my dismay at having to stand for over three hours very quickly disappeared when I realized I was watching a performance by Mark Rylance that was already changing my thoughts on how to play Henry. His playful delivery of the text coupled with a joyful irreverence, which in turn brought out the comedy, was a revelation to me. I had always known that the best way to do Shakespeare was not to be intimidated by it, but I had never watched anyone who so fearlessly and so completely owned the language and made it his. He was technically brilliant, but I only noted that fact afterwards, having realized I had heard every word. A tendency of mine before watching this performance had been to concentrate so much on the clarity of the text that it became a bit sterile. Rylance's Hamlet was funny, spiteful and tragic. It was a performance steeped in complexity and he never shied away from that fact. Despite the heightened language, you never felt lost with him; the audience were invited into all his decision-making. I found him breathtaking – so much so that I can't remember much else about the production. I think I concentrated so much on him because I realized I was being given a masterclass in holding the attention of the audience.

Orphan King

Henry VI, Part I begins with the burial of Henry V. It's a brilliant scene, illustrating one of Shakespeare's greatest strengths: his ability to condense so much dramatic content and information into so little space and time. This statement may seem odd, as Shakespeare is so often shortened in modern productions; but that has more to do with the attention span of contemporary audiences than with Shakespeare. The scene dramatizes the embryonic stages of the in-fighting that eventually causes the loss of France. It also vividly shows the beginning of the end as far as courteous, courtly behaviour is concerned: the Duke of Gloucester (Henry V's brother) and the Bishop of Winchester (Henry V's uncle) have a public argument in front of the funeral party; it's a shocking display of irreverence, which is noted by all present.

To compound the dissension brewing amongst the English gentry, the French, conquered by Henry V not long before his death, are beginning to make headway in regaining their country from the English. Talbot, England's most famous and accomplished war captain, has been captured, and to make matters worse the French have recently acquired their most lethal weapon, Joan of Arc.

Henry VI's being absent till the third act meant that I had a chance to assess what he was up against before I'd even spoken my first line; what was especially useful was being onstage for almost all of the first three acts, as a soldier, so I was involved in the rehearsals of these scenes. Michael's decision to have absolutely everyone, regardless of size of part, playing additional smaller parts meant that from the very start any

9

hint of hierarchy was eradicated. It also created a sense of camaraderie, which in turn created a safe environment in which to experiment.

Although Talbot is released by ransom, Joan of Arc, who claims to be aided by 'Christ's mother', proves to be the inspiration the French need, not only to keep the English at bay but also to start pushing them back. Meanwhile, in England, the wrangling between the lords continues. The power vacuum that Henry V's death creates, combined with the fact that his death leaves an heir of only nine months of age, means that the lords descend like vultures, all jostling for a piece of power. The most robust example of this is played out between Gloucester, the 'Protector' and rightful conductor of the infant King's affairs, and Winchester, the ambitious bishop who wishes to be the power behind the throne.

GLOUCESTER

The Church! Where is it? Had not churchmen pray'd,
His thread of life had not so soon decay'd.
None do you like but an effeminate prince,
Whom, like a school-boy, you may overawe.

WINCHESTER

Gloucester, whate'er we like, thou art Protector,
And lookest to command the Prince and realm.
Thy wife is proud; she holdeth thee in awe
More than God or religious churchmen may.

GLOUCESTER

Name not religion, for thou lov'st the flesh,
And ne'er throughout the year to church thou go'st
Except it be to pray against thy foes.

Left on the stage alone at the end of the scene, Winchester determines:

Each hath his place and function to attend:
I am left out; for me nothing remains;
But long will I not be Jack out of office:
The King from Eltham I intend to steal,
And sit at chiefest stern of public weal.

(Act I, scene i)

If Winchester and Gloucester are the spark for 'The Wars of the Roses', then York emerges as the fire.

'The Wars of the Roses' is the name given to the second tetralogy within the eight-play cycle that makes up Shakespeare's history plays. It all begins in *Richard II* when Richard is wrongfully, or rightfully (depending on whose side you're on), deposed by the future Henry IV. Richard is then murdered in the Tower and, because he has no heir, it leaves the way clear for Henry IV to rule. Henry IV dies years later, after a life racked with guilt at having despatched Richard, leaving his son, Henry V, to rule. What comes to light in *Henry VI, Part I* is that Henry IV not only deposed Richard but was allowed to reign wrongfully, being son to the fourth son of Edward III (who was predecessor to Richard II), whilst the daughter to the third son was overlooked; this third daughter was great-grandmother to York (or 'Richard Plantagenet', as he is entitled at the start of the play). Therefore, since Richard II, the first son of Edward III, had died without an heir, and the second son had died in infancy, York's great-grandmother should have been made queen. These facts had led to York, as his mortal enemy Somerset states in the Temple Garden scene (Act II, scene iv), being 'exempt [excluded] from ancient gentry'. Having discovered these facts from his imprisoned uncle, Mortimer, he vows to reinstate the House of York to the throne.

PLANTAGENET [York]

　　And for those wrongs, those bitter injuries,
　　Which Somerset hath offer'd to my house,
　　I doubt not but with honour to redress;
　　And therefore haste I to the Parliament,
　　Either to be restored to my blood,
　　Or make mine ill th'advantage of my good.

　　　(Act II, scene v)

So, with France on the verge of being lost, his uncles at each other's throats in the pursuit of power, and a legitimate claimant to the throne on the horizon, in walks the infant King in Act III.

'That may well be what actually happened, but . . .'

I had done some research, but not a lot. If I'm honest, this had more to do with laziness than anything else. To my surprise and complete delight, most research would have been pointless. Shakespeare has been so irreverent where history is concerned that any serious research would have just led to confusion; in fact, the little research I had done did just that: confuse me. I remember several conversations with Michael Boyd, ending with him saying, 'That may well be what actually happened, but it's not what Shakespeare has written,' and he was absolutely right.

　　One example of this centred around how old Henry VI should be at different stages of the play. Historical accuracy immediately becomes irrelevant when it transpires that Henry VI was born in 1422, and the argument between Gloucester and Winchester that marks his first scene (Act III, scene i) took place in 1425, making Henry VI supposedly able to demand a truce between his uncles at the age of three. Other examples of Shakespeare's lack of concern with historical accuracy in this play are: Orleans and Rouen were never retaken after being lost to the French; Talbot's visit to the Countess of Auvergne and the plucking of the roses in the Temple Garden are complete fiction; and the demonization of Joan is pure propaganda. Within my research I didn't spot one bit of factual chronology.

Shakespeare's main concern in writing these plays was not to give a history lesson, but to tell compelling stories full of intrigue, love, lust, death, betrayal and above all the insane pursuit of worldly power over spiritual fulfilment.

There's an often-used saying amongst actors: 'Love your character.' I believe the only way you can truly do a character justice is by not judging the character's actions but trying to understand them and then justify them from moment to moment. Of course, this becomes difficult when you're playing a serial killer, but that's why some parts are harder to play than others. Even in the very early stages I noticed that my opinion of what the plays are about differed greatly from the opinions of the other actors; everyone was 'loving his or her character'. Most of the characters within these plays are driven by very separate agendas, and yet they all revolve around the same thing: the acquisition of the Crown. Being the character with the crown on his head meant that my opinions were bound to differ, especially when my character very much felt as if kingship had chosen him rather than him choosing it.

I felt particularly voiceless early on in rehearsals; of twenty-nine actors I was the last to speak. Having seen all the other characters proclaim their agendas, before the King himself had even been seen, made me wonder why the play was called *Henry VI* at all. I would be lying if I said my ego was not slightly bruised by Henry's absence, primarily because, as the weeks went on, I was desperate to make my mark on the play.

I was also unhealthily aware of the pressures of playing a title role. In the past I had longed to get a good mention in a review, but I had largely played parts that by no means guaranteed one. I remember quite clearly the moment I realized that I would definitely be mentioned in every review, for better or for worse – I think I actually broke out in a cold sweat; so I was desperate to start, quite simply to see if I had it in me.

My feelings about Henry's absence changed as rehearsals went on: I began to realize the potential of Shakespeare's set-up. Although we don't see him for two whole acts, he is talked about incessantly – present by his absence; and inevitably the audience's appetite is whetted both by his absence and by being privy to what the child king is going to be up against.

'A Crap King'

One point of constant disagreement between the actors was the degree of intelligence and strength I was to show in the young Henry. I remember an actor responding to Michael's direction for everyone to kneel before me: 'I wouldn't kneel to him; he's a crap king.' In 'loving my character', I could not afford to believe that Henry was a 'crap king' just because the history books say that and so many of the characters within the play say it; after all, Henry VI ruled for almost sixty years, and playing a 'crap king' for three long plays would not be dramatically interesting to me and/or the audience. So, in building Henry, I set out to build a boy, and subsequently a man, who rather than just being a 'crap king' is dealing as best he can with the insurmountable odds surrounding him. Thankfully Michael was of the same opinion as me on this issue; I was constantly able to rely on him monitoring the level of status I was being afforded at any given time. I've heard it said that an actor can't play being royalty; it is a quality given you by those around you. I found this to be true.

One of the first decisions I had to make in playing Henry was how old he should be. With Shakespeare, age tends to be an irrelevant consideration; for instance, you wouldn't expect to see Romeo and Juliet being played as fourteen-year-olds, as is stipulated in the play, and Hamlet is almost never awarded to an actor under the age of thirty, despite the assumption that he must be in his early twenties (or less – a student at Wittenberg University – although confusingly described by the Gravedigger in Act V as thirty). But I was playing a character whose ageing process is pivotal to the narrative.

Historically, Henry was only nine when he was crowned King of France, an event dramatized in Act IV, meaning that Henry is *under* nine when we first see him, in Act III. I knew I couldn't get away with that, so I went for him being about fifteen.

I had made a decision very early on not to use any ageing make-up. One of the compelling things about theatre is how both audience and actors buy into an unreal reality. If an actor says, 'I have thirty thousand soldiers offstage,' the audience accept that. On this principle I didn't see why, if I said I was fifteen, or indeed fifty, years old, the audience would not buy into that. The challenge this decision brought was: how to capture the essence of a very young boy and, later on in the plays, a middle-aged man, without resorting to caricature.

Part of our preparation for breaking into these plays was a series of movement workshops, where we explored elements ranging from the violence of war to the essence of nobility. In the early stages of rehearsals everyone took part in these workshops, because we were frequently soldiers whenever we weren't onstage being our main characters. Not having a single staged fight within a set of plays charting one of the bloodiest chapters in English history was one of the only down sides of playing Henry VI. I loved the war workshops because I knew that, in playing the pacifist King, I wouldn't get to do anything overtly physical.

While still at LAMDA, despite an already punishing schedule, my fight partner and I would spend hours after college perfecting our fight routines in order to win the annual fight competition. We won it twice out of the three years I was there. You can imagine my frustration, therefore, to find that all Henry would ever do with a sword was knight people.

The most useful of these workshops was the investigation of nobility. We played status games using improvisation; for instance, having been put into pairs, we were given different levels of status and a scenario in which one person had to try to get something (information or a possession) from the other person whilst at all times maintaining our different levels of status. These helped to establish a language of nobility and status for the group. This was most important for big court scenes in which social distinction needed to be clear, especially in these plays, where virtually every character is either guarding their status, trying to attain status or on the verge of losing status. Even more useful than the improvisation was investigating the status that had been woven into the language. Lyn Darnley, our voice coach, spent hours with me as we sifted through the clues Shakespeare had given of the emotional arc Henry is on through this play. She opened my eyes to the fact that a rhyming couplet isn't just there to round off a scene, but can also be a powerful tool to demonstrate intent and assurance:

HENRY

When Gloucester says the word, King Henry goes;
For friendly counsel cuts off many foes.

(Act III, scene i)

She also helped me see that when the iambic pentameter breaks down within a speech it sometimes signifies the character's state of mind. She showed me very basic techniques, but they all made a difference. One of the main things I learnt from Lyn was how important it is to ask questions when you don't understand elements within Shakespeare. I had spent three years at LAMDA and never fully understood what iambic pentameter was; in my bid not to look stupid I had spent the first few years of my career pretending to know what it was. When Lyn came along and showed me that it was simply a five-beat rhythm around which verse is written, and how to use that as a help rather than a hindrance, I felt even more stupid, firstly for having shut off every time my drama school teachers taught on it, because I had decided it was a difficult subject; and secondly for having waited so long to find out what it actually was.

Iambic pentameter is one of many things that make Shakespeare, at face value, feel daunting and inaccessible. Early on in rehearsals I realized that a lot of the baggage I was carrying – attitudes and fears about playing Shakespeare – was hindering my ability to simply tell the story. When I finally plucked up the courage to find out what iambic pentameter was, I found it was a bit like the off-side rule in soccer: everyone knows it has something to do with football; not everyone understands it; but once you do, you appreciate the game better.

Henry's first scene is incredibly telling, in that, even though we've waited two acts to see him, he doesn't say a word during the argument that ensues between Winchester and Gloucester; but when he does speak, his words are incisive and full of wisdom:

GLOUCESTER
As good!
Thou bastard of my grandfather!
WINCHESTER
Ay, lordly sir; for what are you, I pray,
But one imperious in another's throne?
GLOUCESTER
Am I not Protector, saucy priest?
WINCHESTER
And am not I a prelate of the church?
GLOUCESTER
Yes, as an outlaw in a castle keeps,
And useth it – to patronage his theft.

WINCHESTER

Unreverent Gloucester!

GLOUCESTER

Thou art reverend

Touching thy spiritual function, not thy life.

WINCHESTER

Rome shall remedy this.

. . .

KING HENRY

Uncles of Gloucester and of Winchester,
The special watchmen of our English weal,
I would prevail, if prayers might prevail,
To join your hearts in love and amity.
O, what a scandal is it to our crown
That two such noble peers as ye should jar!
Believe me, lords, my tender years can tell
Civil dissension is a viperous worm
That gnaws the bowels of the commonwealth.

(Act III, scene i)

Henry's initial absence and subsequent silence at moments of great poignancy were, to begin with, a source of frustration for me, but through them I learned a principle that changed one of my views on acting. A teacher at LAMDA used to say 'acting is all about reacting', and in playing this part I discovered how true this statement was. In young actors like myself, nervous energy and youthful enthusiasm often mean that 'acting' becomes just that: all about doing. Of course, acting is active, which in turn involves doing; but that is only one aspect of it. The illusion of truth created by an actor through 'acting' is dependent on truthful reactions to what is going on around him/her. 'Acting', when not triggered off by reacting, becomes all about doing a part as opposed to being the part. A criticism often levelled at me while at LAMDA was that, I was too technical an actor, my performances were deemed too polished. I now realize that this was because I tended to have every single aspect of my performance meticulously mapped out. By so doing I hadn't made myself as open as I could be to what was happening around me. As human beings we are constantly reacting to our environment; by not adopting this basic human trait onstage an actor's performance can lack humanity and feel contrived.

Henry's youth combined with the weight of responsibility resting on his shoulders means that he is constantly reacting to situations without the wisdom experience brings. Although we see that he deals quite maturely with the first hurdle to confront him, what becomes apparent is that he is totally unaware of the depth of feeling and malicious intent behind what he would call irresponsible bickering.

A Very Lonely Figure

In rehearsals I had this theory that Henry's ineptitude in matters of politics was to do with an upbringing that didn't involve either parent. Although we see Henry's mother Katherine in *Henry V*, there is no mention of her in *Henry VI*. I abandoned this theory in the light of the fact that the Duke of Gloucester emerges as the father figure Henry lacks. If anything, it's not until the second and third parts of this trilogy that being an orphan king begins to take its toll; but the fact remains: Henry is a very lonely figure within this play. Shakespeare makes much of this fact by creating scenes like Act III, scene i (Henry's first scene), in which he is acknowledged as King, though he is all but ignored. Michael highlighted this loneliness by having me enter this scene unaccompanied, tentatively sit on the throne and wait to be joined by the court, who then entered, but not before the audience had had time to take in the much-talked-about boy King.

Gloucester, having been appointed Lord Protector, is the only character, except for the absent Talbot, who has the King's interests at heart. This fact leads to a beautiful relationship being played out between Henry and Gloucester. The investigation of this relationship was one of the most enjoyable aspects of the rehearsal process for me. Richard Cordery (the actor playing Gloucester) and I had worked together during my first season at the RSC. This proved to be an invaluable help in accessing the depth of feeling these two characters have for each other.

One of strangest things about being an actor is how quickly you are expected to portray intimacy with someone you don't know. Stories of arriving on a film set at 7 a.m. and being in bed with someone you've only just met by 8 a.m. are common. Thankfully, this is not the case in theatre, where having a rehearsal period means that actors are afforded time to achieve a level of intimacy between their characters that is believable. Tools such as improvisation, role-playing, conversation and, above all, rehearsal help to lessen the awkwardness that can sometimes hinder the exploration of the characters, their relationships and the play. Already knowing Richard Cordery meant we had a head start.

Gloucester's fondness for the King is illustrated through the argument between Gloucester and Winchester at the top of Act III:

WINCHESTER

He shall submit, or I will never yield.

GLOUCESTER

Compassion on the King commands me stoop,
Or I would see his heart out, ere the priest
Should ever get that privilege of me.

WARWICK

Behold, my Lord of Winchester, the Duke
Hath banish'd moody discontented fury,
As by his smoothed brows it doth appear:
Why look you still so stern and tragical?

GLOUCESTER

Here, Winchester, I offer thee my hand.

(Act III, scene i)

The scene ends with the alliance between the King and Gloucester being very apparent. Warwick and Gloucester support the reinstatement of York to 'ancient gentry' – his family's former titles – and Gloucester suggests that the time is right for the King to 'be crown'd in France', with both of which

Henry immediately complies. I took special delight in the Gloucester–Henry relationship because I was aware that it would be my only opportunity within the three Henry VI plays to explore requited love. Henry and Gloucester are never at any point dishonest with each other – the exact opposite of Henry's involvement with nearly every other character except Talbot.

Talbot's character emerges as the embodiment of everything England once was; he acts as the barometer by which honour and loyalty are measured, especially in relation to all the other characters. Indeed, the fact that Talbot comes out of this play feeling a bit old-fashioned and other-worldly bears this out. He fought alongside Henry V and worships his memory. He has no time for Machiavelli. Gloucester's loyalty and the honour of Talbot make them the only characters Henry truly admires. We see this in Act III, scene iv when, on the way to being crowned in France, Henry, accompanied by Gloucester and their party, meets Talbot:

KING HENRY

Is this the Talbot, uncle Gloucester,
That hath so long been resident in France?

GLOUCESTER

Yes, if it please your Majesty, my liege.

KING HENRY

Welcome, brave captain and victorious lord!
When I was young, as yet I am not old,
I do remember how my father said
A stouter champion never handled sword.
Long since we were resolved of your truth,
Your faithful service, and your toil in war;
Yet never have you tasted our reward,
Or been reguerdon'd with so much as thanks,

Because till now we never saw your face.
Therefore stand up; and for these good deserts
We here create you Earl of Shrewsbury;
And in our coronation take your place.

This scene proved to be one in which I could show the childish side of Henry. It was staged so that the lords and I arrived on a balcony above the stage, looking down on Talbot as he arrived. After the formal introductions had been made, Michael had me climbing down from the balcony in a rush of excitement to meet my hero. He had asked me to imagine that I had posters of 'The Great Talbot' up on my bedroom wall. This image helped to bring out the undignified hero-worship of a small boy – a revealing contrast to the Henry we'd seen in his last scene, where he was forced to be grown-up and take charge.

One of the most difficult things I found in building Henry in *Part I* was how little stage time I had to illustrate the complexity of the character. I soon realized that my frustration stemmed from having read *Parts II* and *III*; I was pre-empting, i.e. playing the end of the trilogy at the beginning of the first play. Looking back now, I can see that a lot of what I had acquired in knowledge of the character by the end of rehearsing *Parts II* and *III* then fed back; but it was wrong to try to pack it all in at the beginning.

The other trap I fell into briefly was trying to bring out the subtext. In Shakespeare, characters always say what they mean; if they lie to another character, the audience will find this out either in an aside or during a confession of the lie to another character. These discoveries released me into being simpler with my exploration of Henry. What I subsequently found was that, in playing this orphaned boy King living in the shadow of his war-god father whilst being thrust to the helm of this sinking ship, England, I had more than enough material to be getting on with without creating subtext.

I have heard it said, and I now agree, that there is no subtext in Shakespeare, because he gives you everything you need to build the character in the words. Having said that, what then happens is that subtext grows out of doing the play night after night. The relationship played out between Henry and Gloucester felt so much richer after six months of doing the play than at the beginning of the run. There were elements we had built in that Shakespeare hadn't necessarily written, but which we had built on to the foundation of what he had written. Shakespeare's ability to pack so much meaning into an individual line, let alone one of his major characters, means that they become almost inexhaustible sources of exploration and depth.

Having got over my frustration at Henry's lack of airtime in *Part I*, I soon began to enjoy unravelling the complexity of both his character and his situation. Every new scene seemed to present a different aspect of his personality; for instance, in Act III, scene i we see Henry being assertive, and then, in Act III, scene iv, we see him being childish. The investigation of each scene and the given obstacle Henry is presented with helped me in building a three-dimensional character. Human beings are full of contradictions, and for an actor those contradictions are what makes a character compelling to play. More than with any character I had formerly played, I found myself better able to understand and play the contradictions that dwelt within Henry the further into the play we ploughed.

Henry's Achilles Heel: The Red and the White

My next scene (Act IV, scene i) was my favourite, partly because it's Henry's biggest scene in the play, but also because in it so much happens to him and so many aspects of his personality are revealed. Before the scene is over he has shown anxiety, courage, insecurity, naivety, pride and doubt. It was a golden opportunity to propel the character forward. The scene starts with Henry being crowned King of France. It's a terrifying moment for him; he is literally stepping into the legacy of his famous father. Henry being crowned King of England is not dramatized in the play, so seeing the boy King being crowned King of France becomes a poignant moment. The designer made a masterstroke in choosing to put me in a robe that looked too big and ill-fitting, in order to emphasize Henry's state of mind.

The coronation was staged beautifully; all the nobles, adorned with silver robes and upturned swords, preceded my entrance. I was then escorted in by Gloucester, who ushered me through a corridor of nobles towards Winchester, whose task it was to place the crown on my head. All of this was underscored by slow and rib-cage-jarringly loud drumbeats. This point in the play was always quite emotional for me in an almost inexplicable way. I often couldn't believe how fortunate I was to be living out a daydream I had often had, but I also felt there were those in the audience who were in just as much disbelief at the fact that the RSC would let a black man be crowned on the famous Swan stage. Indeed, the very first newspaper article that announced my acquisition of the part quoted an Oxford University don as saying: 'We should aim to be accurate in our representation of the text. Moves like these leave us open to ridicule. King Henry VI wasn't black and shouldn't be cast as such.'*

I had heard of a production of *Henry V* – I think at the RSC – where a black actor was playing the French king. As he made his entrance, an audience member was heard to say, 'This is a disgrace,' before very publicly making their exit. Whether this story is true or not, I don't know, but it flashed through my mind every time I did this scene.

I remember being astonished at the number of obstacles Henry has to face before the scene is over. His crowning is immediately followed by a messenger arriving in the form of a deserter, whom he immediately banishes, but not before his message is relayed. The message is then revealed to announce yet another desertion, that of the Duke of Burgundy, who, although French, has been one of England's greatest allies against France. This news immediately puts England's hold on France into the balance. For me this proved to be the perfect moment, in mapping Henry's development, to begin the transition from boy to man. Henry orders his hero Talbot to seek out Burgundy and bring him to justice:

KING HENRY

What! doth my uncle Burgundy revolt?

GLOUCESTER

He doth, my lord, and is become your foe.

KING HENRY

Is that the worst this letter doth contain?

GLOUCESTER

It is the worst, and all, my lord, he writes.

KING HENRY

Why then Lord Talbot there shall talk with him

* *Daily Telegraph.*

And give him chastisement for this abuse.
My lord, how say you, are you not content?

TALBOT

Content, my liege! Yes, but that I am prevented,
I should have begg'd I might have been employ'd.

KING HENRY

Then gather strength and march unto him straight;
Let him perceive how ill we brook his treason,
And what offence it is to flout his friends.

TALBOT

I go, my lord, in heart desiring still
You may behold confusion of your foes.

These instructions are immediately followed by the presentation of a dispute between two lords, who 'crave the benefit of law of arms'. The two lords are followers of the arch-rivals York and Somerset; both lords claim their grievance stems from the other showing disrespect for their respective masters. This escalates into York and Somerset defending their respective allies to the point of combat, which is then curtailed by Gloucester:

GLOUCESTER

Presumptuous vassals, are you not asham'd
With this immodest clamorous outrage
To trouble and disturb the King and us?
And you, my lords, methinks you do not well
To bear with their perverse objections,
Much less to take occasion from their mouths
To raise a mutiny betwixt yourselves:
Let me persuade you take a better course.

Taking his lead from Gloucester, we then hear Henry deliver the most robust reprimand of the court that he gives at any point in all three plays. The speech in which he does this posed a new challenge for me, namely, delivering a long Shakespearean speech. Long speeches in general can be an actor's making or undoing – making, partly because, if every actor were honest, they'd admit to loving the undivided attention of the audience, and the power that affords them; undoing, because that attention very quickly fades if they haven't conquered the speech, by which I mean reached such a level of understanding of the speech that they can truly play it, exactly as a musician would bring their personality to a piece, having rigorously mastered it. This is especially true with Shakespeare, whose language is alien to the modern ear and whose speeches are often packed full of symbolism, wit and exposition.

The RSC have some of the best voice teachers, and it was Lyn Darnley who continually dragged me away from my bad habits, which included lack of clarity, not using the antithesis and simply not using clues Shakespeare has put there to help you unlock a speech.

Henry begins his 'persuasion speech' by dealing with the current altercation between York and Somerset at source:

Come hither, you that would be combatants:
Henceforth I charge you, as you love our favour,
Quite to forget this quarrel, and the cause.

He then shows an acute awareness of the fragility of the hold England has on France, whilst highlighting that this is exactly the wrong time for in-fighting:

And you, my lords, remember where we are:
In France, amongst a fickle wavering nation;
If they perceive dissension in our looks,
And that within ourselves we disagree,

> How will their grudging stomachs be provok'd
> To wilful disobedience, and rebel!

Henry's misjudgement of the depth of this quarrel is then revealed by his reference to it being over a 'toy, a thing of no regard':

> Beside, what infamy will there arise
> When foreign princes shall be certified
> That for *a toy, a thing of no regard,*
> King Henry's peers and chief nobility
> Destroy'd themselves, and lost the realm of France!

Henry's Achilles heel throughout these plays is his failure to fully understand the nature of what is going on in his own court. His lack of exposure to court intrigue, and his naive assumption that his courtiers all adhere to the same guidebook as he does, the Bible, leave him perpetually behind the game. With Henry, I kept feeling as if he was the right king at the wrong time. In a time of peace, with the right kind of influence, his reign's potential feels endless.

When I was younger, I was convinced that war was completely senseless and unnecessary; I could never understand the words 'winning' and 'losing' being used in reference to the loss of so many lives. I had a theory that the leaders of the opposing countries should simply play a game of chess; it would save all that destruction, and the terms 'winning' or 'losing' could still be used – naive I know, but it's an idealistic notion that I can almost imagine Henry embracing.

Even though his referring to the 'red' and 'white' as things 'of no regard' is a political blunder, there is an undeniable truth about these rose symbols (as emblems of the warring Houses of York and Lancaster) becoming ultimately destructive to the common good of England. What Henry fails to realize is that they are just that: symbols, beyond which much greater feelings lie.

The following part of the speech left me with quite an important character choice to make:

> O, think upon the conquest of my father,
> My tender years, and let us not forgo
> That for a trifle that was bought with blood!
> Let me be umpire in this doubtful strife.

The problem was: in mentioning his father and his own youth, is Henry being manipulative or sincere? The more we rehearsed, the more apparent it became that choices like this were crucial for getting the character right. I remember, early in rehearsals, playing it as completely sincere; I later chose to play it as emotional blackmail. Of course, this wasn't something to be displayed overtly, but the seed thought was enough to give the speech a complex dynamic. It meant that I could start building Henry as a potentially brilliant politician – again, far more interesting than playing the end of the plays at the beginning.

In referring to his father's achievement in acquiring France and the horror that its loss would be, he brings up the only fact on which the whole court is agreed; but, as always with Henry, he can't seem to separate political reality from moral ideology:

> I see no reason, if I wear this rose, [*Putting on a red rose.*]
> That any one should therefore be suspicious
> I more incline to Somerset than York:
> Both are my kinsmen, and I love them both;
> As well may they upbraid me with my crown,
> Because, forsooth, the King of Scots is crown'd.

It is his ideology that sets him apart, and it became the most rewarding aspect of this character to play. I so enjoyed playing a character who was constantly swimming against the tide. In the face of insurmountable odds he never loses faith in God, or the human spirit.

> But your discretions better can persuade
> Than I am able to instruct or teach;
> And therefore, as we hither came in peace,
> So let us still continue peace and love.
> Cousin of York, we institute your Grace
> To be our Regent in these parts of France:
> And, good my Lord of Somerset, unite
> Your troops of horsemen with his bands of foot;
> And like true subjects, sons of your progenitors,
> Go cheerfully together and digest.
> Your angry choler on your enemies.
> Ourself, my Lord Protector, and the rest,
> After some respite will return to Calais;
> From thence to England, where I hope ere long
> To be presented by your victories
> With Charles, Alençon and that traitorous rout.

This speech, certainly on those days when we performed all three *Henrys* on the same day, proved to be a watershed. My instinct was that physically seeing him crowned had to be a poignant moment within the story structure.

Within these plays 'the crown' represents so much:

KING RICHARD

> Doubly divorc'd! Bad men, you violate
> A twofold marriage – 'twixt my crown and me,
> And then betwixt me and my married wife.
>
> (*King Richard II*, Act V, scene i)

KING [HENRY IV]

> God knows, my son,

By what by-paths and indirect crook'd ways
I met this crown; and I myself know well
How troublesome it sat upon my head.

(*Henry IV, Part II*, Act IV, scene v)

KING [HENRY V]

Not today, O Lord,
O not today, think not upon the fault
My father made in compassing the crown.

(*King Henry V*, Act IV, scene i)

KING [HENRY VI]

My crown is in my heart, not on my head;
Not decked with diamonds and Indian stones,
Nor to be seen; my crown is called content;
A crown it is that seldom kings enjoy.

(*Henry VI, Part III*, Act III, scene i)

The irony of the crown being an object lusted after by many yet one in the possession of which few find happiness is twofold, when we see a godly man upon whom the crown is thrust. Through his birth he is deemed God's chosen one; yet the reality of kingship for him is that he has unwittingly signed a Faustian pact, beyond which all hell breaks loose. It's no coincidence that within seconds of his being crowned we see Henry having to deal with foreign as well as domestic affairs that are direct or indirect challenges to his right to the crown.

A source of constant fascination in the history plays is what the crown represents to different characters. As people, we all occasionally fall prey to the notion that happiness lies within things we don't possess, the difference being that the characters within this play are prepared to kill for it.

The French and the English

Assuming the premise that drama does not exist without conflict, I made the decision that it would not be dramatically interesting to play Henry as a 'bad king'. No one sets out to be a bad anything; their 'badness', or ineptitude, is revealed to them through their unsuccessful attempts at things.

Before rehearsals began I delved into theatrical archives to read about former productions of the Henry plays and, having read the plays, I was surprised to see how many productions had fallen into the trap of portraying Henry as a monkish, anaemic and sullen figure. One of the easiest errors to make, especially with a set of plays that span sixty years, is to pre-empt parts of the narrative through your knowledge of the character and story. The evidence for Henry's spiritual awakening and the solidification of his philosophy of life and rule is only burgeoning in *Part I*. It does the dramatic tension a disservice to have Henry opting out of the political cut and thrust as early as *Part I*. The drama only comes if there is a plausible enough regime against which the pretenders to the throne can fight. Therefore I chose to play 'the persuasion speech' as strongly as I could, to raise the political stakes.

Keeping the political stakes high was something Michael Boyd had to keep a keen eye on. Letting the stakes drop within these highly charged political plays is fatal. Within *Henry VI, Part I* the danger spots were the numerous battleground and political stand-offs that take place between the French and the English, which can feel repetitive. Shakespeare overcomes this by giving each one of these events a very different function within the narrative; our job as the storytellers was to decide on what these were, and to convey it to the audience.

There were instances in rehearsal when it took several weeks to understand the function of a scene; the French scenes were particularly difficult. Firstly, there are fewer of them than the English scenes and they are less detailed, which makes building three-dimensional characters more challenging. Also, in pandering to the propaganda of his day, Shakespeare has deliberately painted the French court (with the exception of Joan) as buffoons. The difficulty that arises is that it becomes hard to understand why England is struggling to keep France.

Michael's vigilance maintained the balance between the genuine threat of the French army under Joan of Arc and the comic relief supplied by the Dauphin's French court – the point, again, being that drama does not exist if the obstacles you are fighting against are not plausible.

Having played Act IV, scene i as forcefully as I could, my next scene then presented the opportunity to uncover yet another piece of Henry's tapestry. Act V, scene i begins with Henry receiving news from Gloucester that 'the Pope, / The Emperor, and the Earl of Armagnac' desire 'To have a godly peace concluded of / Between the realms of England and of France.' This news is, of course, a source of joy to the pacifist King, but yet again Henry's joy is short-lived. One of the conditions of this pact of peace turns out to be an arranged marriage between him and the Earl of Armagnac's daughter. We are promptly reminded that although Henry, when called upon, can chastise his intimidating court, he is still only a young teenager.

GLOUCESTER
    Beside, my lord, the sooner to effect

And surer bind this knot of amity,
The Earl of Armagnac, near knit to Charles,
A man of great authority in France,
Proffers his only daughter to your Grace
In marriage, with a large and sumptuous dowry.

KING HENRY

Marriage, uncle! Alas, my years are young!
And fitter is my study and my books
Than wanton dalliance with a paramour.

Bearing in mind that, between Henry's last scene and this scene, we have witnessed the demise of Talbot, Henry is now at one of his loneliest moments. Talbot is no more, and Gloucester is encouraging a marriage Henry is averse to. Under the sheer weight of respect he has for Gloucester and the realization that he must serve his country first and himself second, he relents.

KING HENRY

Yet call th' ambassadors, and, as you please,
So let them have their answers every one.
I shall be well content with any choice
Tends to God's glory and my country's weal.

This scene also presented one of the only opportunities to show the domestic as opposed to the public face of the Henry–Gloucester relationship. It was imperative that this be clearly painted for the audience – so that its decimation in *Part II* carries the right weight. Michael's keen eye was called upon again in monitoring the relationship. As I've mentioned, Richard Cordery and I had previously worked together, making it easier to access the relationship between our characters, and although this was a huge help, it also proved to be a hindrance: I became more and more guilty of overemphasizing the love they share, to the point of indulgence.

Slipping into indulgence is an accusation often levelled at actors, but it's very easily done. When you are in the middle of building a character, as far as you are concerned you are the centre of your own world, but 'The play's the thing,' and it's the director's job to keep all the actors telling the whole story rather than just their own. The trap I fell into was to be sentimental in the expression of my affection for Gloucester. To my own detriment, I fought Michael on this for several weeks. I was convinced that I was right and that he had become overly obsessed with keeping every ounce of sentiment out of the show.

After several weeks of holding my ground on this issue, I decided to humour Michael, if only to show him how wrong he was. To my utter disappointment, it resulted in all my scenes with Richard being much improved. One of the manifestations of my leaning towards sentimentality was incessant physical contact with Richard. Being denied this crutch meant that I was released to explore – wanting that level of contact with my surrogate father and yet having to find other means of expressing it; and also dealing with the loneliness that ensues from not being allowed to express love. Furthermore, I hadn't taken account of the fact that Richard was six foot four inches, and not exactly skinny, and I was five foot nine, which, since we were playing in the round, meant that every time I went near him half the audience couldn't see me.

I realized how counterproductive it is to lock a scene down and feel as if you've conquered it. The best and most memorable scenes within our productions were the ones that were constantly changing; these tended to be the bigger scenes, in which lots of characters were interacting. I suppose their freshness stemmed from the fact that there were so many people in them – that, inevitably, someone would do something different and that in turn would spin the scene into a new, exciting or (on the odd occasion) disastrous direction; but at least the scenes stayed fresh.

An inevitable side effect of performing the same piece over and over again is that you begin to form patterns. Whenever this happened to me, I found myself pre-empting the action within the scene, which resulted in my performance being less truthful.

The notion of truth in theatre is an odd one, because ultimately theatre is an exercise in buying into a lie. You will often hear actors saying, 'That didn't feel truthful,' of a performance they've given. When I find myself saying this, it's often because I have felt myself to be outside my character, rather than inhabiting his thoughts and therefore his words. With me, this has often stemmed from complacency and feeling as if I was so on top of the part that I could afford to relax a bit, which invariably leads to a lower level of concentration.

Concentration and the sustaining of it are indispensable in relation to the political nature of these plays. If the actor loses the thread of what is happening, inevitably so do the audience. Losing your audience, with Shakespeare, is fatal, and the heightened nature of the language makes it difficult to win them back; you can really feel it when you've lost them. Also, because I didn't feature frequently in *Part I*, there was a premium on not letting the energy that had already been created on stage drop.

The ability to hit the stage powerfully and not let the momentum drop was a skill this play helped me develop. During my first season with the RSC, I had just seven lines in *Antony and Cleopatra*, and I used to get more nervous about doing those lines than I subsequently did before going on to do one of Henry's soliloquies. This was simply because the

39

prospect of messing up my lines when I only had seven of them was bad enough, but it's also a bit like watching a tennis match and being asked in the middle of a long rally to take a shot quickly and hand the racket back. You simply can't afford to let the ball drop.

Margaret

Before the final scene, we see the Duke of Suffolk, who is in France fighting to win back the French crown, fall in lust with the French Lady Margaret and subsequently promise to make her the Queen of England.

'The wooing scene' (Act V, scene iii) is an example of how Shakespeare's writing gives the actor clues as to how to play the scene.

SUFFOLK [*Aside*]
　She's beautiful, and therefore to be woo'd;
　She is a woman, therefore to be won.

MARGARET
　Wilt thou accept of ransom, yea or no?

SUFFOLK
　Fond man, remember that thou hast a wife;
　Then how can Margaret be thy paramour?

MARGARET
　'Twere best to leave him, for he will not hear.

SUFFOLK
　There all is marr'd; there lies a cooling card.

MARGARET
　He talks at random; sure, the man is mad.

SUFFOLK
　And yet a dispensation may be had.

MARGARET
　And yet I would that you would answer me.

SUFFOLK
　I'll win this Lady Margaret. For whom?

Why, for my king! Tush, that's a wooden thing!

MARGARET

He talks of wood: it is some carpenter.

SUFFOLK

Yet so my fancy may be satisfied,
And peace established between these realms.
But there remains a scruple in that too;
For though her father be the King of Naples,
Duke of Anjou and Maine, yet is he poor,
And our nobility will scorn the match.

MARGARET

Hear ye, captain, are you not at leisure?

SUFFOLK

It shall be so, disdain they ne'er so much;
Henry is youthful and will quickly yield. –
Madam, I have a secret to reveal.

MARGARET

What though I be enthrall'd? He seems a knight,
And will not any way dishonour me.

SUFFOLK

Lady, vouchsafe to listen what I say.

MARGARET

Perhaps I shall be rescu'd by the French;
And then I need not crave his courtesy.

SUFFOLK

Sweet madam, give me hearing in a cause –

MARGARET

Tush, women have been captivate ere now.

SUFFOLK

Lady, wherefore talk you so?

MARGARET

I cry you mercy, 'tis but *quid* for *quo*.

Watching this scene in rehearsals was a real learning experience; asides, rhyming couplets and double entendres are all utilized, and they were all elements of Shakespeare I hadn't fully explored. Through watching the scene rehearsed, it became obvious that every one of these elements required complete confidence and commitment on the actor's part.

Asides work only when the actor completely disengages from the scene, addresses the audience and then snaps back into the action. They are invariably used to divulge to the audience a truth or intention that the character does not wish to be known by the other characters. As a result, the execution of an aside requires dexterity of thought and intention: if it is done without real conviction and intent it can leave the audience confused. My attitude to asides before seeing them used so successfully by the actors playing Suffolk and Margaret, was that they were corny and disruptive to the naturalistic style actors of my generation tend to embrace; but the same attitude one must have towards asides is the one to be had towards rhyming couplets, which is to embrace them as a help rather than a hindrance. Rhyming couplets help to establish the relationship between characters very quickly; for instance, they are used to establish the compatibility of Suffolk and Margaret. They can also at times be used to signify a character meeting his/her match, as we see earlier in the play between Talbot and his young son:

TALBOT

Shall all thy mother's hopes lie in one tomb?

JOHN

Ay, rather than I'll shame my mother's womb.

TALBOT

Upon my blessing, I command thee go.

JOHN

To fight I will, but not to fly the foe.

TALBOT

Part of thy father may be sav'd in thee.

JOHN

No part of him but will be sham'd in me.

TALBOT

Thou never hadst renown, nor canst not lose it.

JOHN

Yes, your renowned name: shall flight abuse it?

TALBOT

Thy father's charge shall clear thee from that stain.

JOHN

You cannot witness for me, being slain.
If death be so apparent, then both fly.

TALBOT

And leave my followers here to fight and die?
My age was never tainted with such shame.

JOHN

And shall my youth be guilty of such blame?
No more can I be sever'd from your side
Than can yourself yourself in twain divide.
Stay, go, do what you will, the like do I;
For live I will not, if my father die.

TALBOT

Then here I take my leave of thee, fair son,
Born to eclipse thy life this afternoon.
Come, side by side together live and die,
And soul with soul from France to heaven fly.

(Act IV, scene v)

The meeting of Suffolk and Margaret marks the beginning of an awful chapter in Henry's life, which goes on to span the rest of his days. Suffolk, having been fairly inconspicuous for the duration of the play, suddenly emerges in the fifth act with the most inventive and audacious means of obtaining power we have yet seen. What makes it even more opportunistic is that he seems to stumble upon it. Within the scene we see him fall for Margaret, acknowledge both the fact that he is married and that an affair would be a bad idea, then turn on a sixpence and promise Margaret the King's hand in marriage, whilst not betraying the fact that he has no say in the King's marital affairs. Prompted partly by her father's consent but largely by her own as yet unrealized ambition, as well as by her attraction to Suffolk, she agrees to his proposition.

One of Michael Boyd's masterstrokes in directing these plays was his decision to cast the actress (Fiona Bell) playing Joan of Arc as the future Queen Margaret, too. This was not an easy feat, considering that it required some rearranging of scenes and a ridiculously quick costume change. Michael joined the capture of Joan ('La Pucelle') (Act V, scene iii) to the burning scene (Act V, scene iv) by taking the wooing scene between Suffolk and Margaret (also Act V, scene iii), which followed straight on from the capture of Joan, and placing it after Act V, scene iv. This meant that we saw Joan get burnt at the stake and then re-emerge as Margaret through her own smoke.

Michael's idea to have any actor whose character had died re-emerge as a new character but retain the philosophy of their former incarnation (i.e. remain a Lancastrian or a Yorkist) meant that, even though nearly every actor played more than one character, the audience were never lost as to where their allegiance lay. The idea behind having the actress playing Joan re-emerge as Margaret was so that the audience would make a connection between these two characters, who both in their own ways are England's nemesis.

45

Though the audience saw numerous characters flashing across the stage, instead of getting more lost the more characters they saw, the effect was rather that they felt as if they knew something about a new character because of the actor playing him/her. It was also so much more satisfying for the actors who had multiple parts, to be able to chart a journey through the course of the three plays despite playing more than one character.

Having Joan burnt and then reincarnated as Margaret highlighted the numerous similarities between the two characters that come to light in *Part II*, both being dominant women in a male-dominated environment, both being French and loathed by the English for it, both becoming obsessed by power and it proving to be their undoing, and both having the ability to beguile, as seen in the similarity between the beguilement of Burgundy by Joan and the seduction of Suffolk by Margaret:

BURGUNDY [*Aside*]

    I am vanquished; these haughty words of hers
    Have batter'd me like roaring cannon-shot
    And made me almost yield upon my knees. –
    Forgive me, country, and sweet countrymen!
    And, lords, accept this hearty kind embrace.
    My forces and my power of men are yours.
    So farewell, Talbot; I'll no longer trust thee.

      (Act III, scene iii)

SUFFOLK

    O, wert thou for myself! But, Suffolk, stay;
    Thou may'st not wander in that labyrinth:
    There Minotaurs and ugly treasons lurk.
    Solicit Henry with her wondrous praise.
    Bethink thee on her virtues that surmount,

And natural graces that extinguish art;
Repeat their semblance often on the seas,
That, when thou com'st to kneel at Henry's feet,
Thou may'st bereave him of his wits with wonder.

(Act V, scene iii)

Suffolk's exploits with Margaret are followed by York's begrudgingly made treaty of peace with France and, with this juxtaposition, the audience are now privy to the conflict arising in the last scene of the play. Henry is torn between lust and duty: between, on the one hand, Margaret's beauty, among other qualities, as told to him by Suffolk; and, on the other, his loyalty to Gloucester, requiring that he secure peace between England and France by an arranged marriage to the Earl of Armagnac's daughter. Michael and I disagreed on how this scene should begin. He was keen for Margaret to appear in the form of a portrait during the course of the scene. This wouldn't have bothered me so much if it had just been an ordinary painting, but it was a huge golden frame, to be lowered from the rafters of the very high Swan Theatre, with Fiona Bell in it. I initially suppressed my feelings, aware that it doesn't aid creativity to quash an idea before it has been explored, and that my ego was probably reacting to the prospect of being upstaged by a descending golden frame; but the more we rehearsed the scene, the more I felt that my original instincts had been right. Michael's staging had Henry and Suffolk storming in on a wave of jocular enthusiasm generated by Suffolk's recounting of Margaret's innumerable good qualities.

KING HENRY

Your wondrous rare description, noble Earl,
Of beauteous Margaret hath astonish'd me:
Her virtues, graced with external gifts

Do breed love's settled passions in my heart:
And like as rigour of tempestuous gusts
Provokes the mightiest hulk against the tide,
So am I driven by breath of her renown
Either to suffer shipwreck, or arrive
Where I may have fruition of her love.

(Act V, scene v)

It was during this speech that the portrait of Margaret descended into view. I was concerned that, as the frame was lowered, inevitably the audience wouldn't focus on a word I was saying, and the crucial speech that followed – one in which Suffolk's talent for persuasive oratory is demonstrated – would also be marginalized.

SUFFOLK

The chief perfections of that lovely dame,
Had I sufficient skill to utter them,
Would make a volume of enticing lines,
Able to ravish any dull conceit;
And, which is more, she is not so divine,
So full replete with choice of all delights,
But with a humble lowliness of mind
She is content to be at your command;
Command, I mean, of virtuous chaste intents,
To love and honour Henry as her lord.

I felt that the actor playing Suffolk was robbed of a piece of the jigsaw that could go towards building his performance. Surely the point of this section of the scene was that Henry was being seduced primarily by Suffolk, a by-product of which was an allegiance being formed that threatened Gloucester's position. Michael and I discussed this several times before and during the run of the production. Part of me felt that I was being unreasonable, but equally I felt that the creation of a pretty picture was taking precedence over clear storytelling. With time, rather than fighting it, I embraced this moment in the play and it became absorbed into the journey of my character. It illustrated to me how difficult it must be for a director to strike a balance between his/her vision, and all the actors' individual takes on their characters and the story. The fact is that the frame did work, because, in having Margaret so impressively lowered from the ceiling, a clear juxtaposition was made between Margaret and the Earl of Armagnac's daughter, who had been presented to Henry in Act V, scene i in a small golden frame on wheels. By the making of one prospective wife's entrance and regalia more impressive than the other, the audience are pulled into Henry's dilemma and subsequent decision. I still felt it detracted from what was being said onstage, but it's the director's job to decide which bits of the story he/she wants the audience to focus on at any given time, much in the way a film director does during the editing process.

The more we rehearsed this scene, the more I realized how important a scene it was within the trilogy. The defiant decision Henry makes is one that goes on to haunt him both politically and spiritually for the rest of his life. I remember, when I first read the scene, thinking that it was out of character for Henry to make such a rash decision, especially without even seeing the woman. What I hadn't accounted for was that he is a young man barely beyond puberty and on the verge of sexual awakening. As always with Shakespeare, there are several ways to interpret a character, and it became very clear to me that, despite his religious convictions, he was quite simply being human and going for the more attractive girl: 'Her virtues graced with external gifts / Do breed love's settled passions in my heart.'

Henry can't help but mention her 'virtues', but her 'external gifts' are the overriding factor. As the scene progresses, we see Henry relegated to observer of a fierce debate between Gloucester and Suffolk. Both make very valid points as to the pros and cons of a match between Henry and Margaret. Gloucester pushes all the right buttons by talking of Henry honouring his promise to the Earl of Armagnac's daughter, calling Margaret's father, Reignier, a charlatan and citing the political advantages of uniting with the house of Armagnac. Suffolk is just as convincing in reminding Henry that one of the privileges of being king is one's rite to break 'unlawful oaths'; he also endows Margaret's father with as much political status as the Earl of Armagnac. Exeter then makes a statement that severely threatens Suffolk's cause: 'Reignier sooner will receive than give'.

Henry's belief in God is a side of him explored in more detail in *Parts II* and *III* of this trilogy; none the less, we see it being established in this play. Henry is well versed in biblical teaching; he would immediately recognize Exeter's reference to Acts 20:35 – 'It is more blessed to give than to receive.' Suffolk recognizes the danger and pulls out his ace card; he talks of love:

A dower, my lords! Disgrace not so your king,
That he should be so abject, base, and poor,
To choose for wealth and not for perfect love.
Henry is able to enrich his queen,
And not to seek a queen to make him rich:
So worthless peasants bargain for their wives,
As market-men for oxen, sheep, or horse.
Marriage is a matter of more worth
Than to be dealt in by attorneyship;
Not whom we will, but whom his Grace affects,
Must be companion of his nuptial bed;

And therefore, lords, since he affects her most,
[That] most of all these reasons bindeth us
In our opinions she should be preferr'd.
For what is wedlock forced but a hell,
An age of discord and continual strife?
Whereas the contrary bringeth bliss,
And is a pattern of celestial peace.
Whom should we match with Henry, being a king,
But Margaret, that is daughter to a king?
Her peerless feature, joined with her birth,
Approves her fit for none but for a king:
Her valiant courage and undaunted spirit,
More than in women commonly is seen,
Will answer our hope in issue of a king;
For Henry, son unto a conqueror,
Is likely to beget more conquerors,
If with a lady of so high resolve
As is fair Margaret he be link'd in love.
Then yield, my lords; and here conclude with me
That Margaret shall be Queen, and none but she.

Suffolk's eulogizing about the virtue of putting love before duty, a notion that appeals to Henry's romantic ideals, gives Henry enough ammunition to justify disobeying both his conscience and his beloved uncle. Henry's mind is made up and he allows no one else to speak until he has instructed Suffolk to fetch Margaret, urged Gloucester to understand his decision on the basis that Gloucester would have done the same if he had been as in love and as young as he is, and then exits, but not before declaring the state of 'grief' he will be in until Margaret's arrival.

This is Henry's final appearance in *Part I* of the trilogy. In performance, having exited, I would always peek through the curtain in order to witness the rest of this scene; I loved the way Michael chose to stage it. After Henry exited, Gloucester scowled at Suffolk and then stormed off, leaving Suffolk to declare his plan to rule England through the future queen:

Thus Suffolk hath prevail'd; and thus he goes,
As did the youthful Paris once to Greece;
With hope to find the like event in love,
But prosper better than the Trojan did.
Margaret shall now be Queen, and rule the King;
But I will rule both her, the King, and realm.

Having essentially said 'To be continued' to the audience, Suffolk exited, leaving the portrait of Margaret which then came to life and she exited, but not before declaring through a simple look in her eyes that things might not run quite as Suffolk intends. The main reason I loved hanging back to watch that ending was to see the wave of disappointment and anticipation that rippled through the audience as they realized that the lights were going down and they would have to wait till *Part II* to see what happens.

One of Michael's greatest strengths as a director is his ability to create visual images that clarify the narrative. The success we experienced with these shows was largely down to Michael's clear storytelling through the spoken word, images and music. The way the music was developed during the rehearsals for these shows was a revelation to me. I had always thought of a theatrical score in filmic terms – as an element added after the play is nearly or fully formed. We had a composer who was present at every rehearsal, and who literally constructed the music of the show around the mood and the movement created by the actors at any given time. In productions I had done in the past, I had found myself seduced into altering my performance to accommodate an imposed musical score. By having a score built around the actors' performances as they were being created, a kind of synergy took place whereby the score became part of the actors' performance. For instance, all of the major characters had their own theme music: mine was a high-pitched sound created by running a violin bow along a woodcutting saw.

The unusual instruments recruited to create the score made for a timeless feel, which was reflected in the costumes and weaponry. Each musical detail was designed to move the story forward, from a finger being run round a half-full wineglass to warn of dark supernatural forces at work, to the rib-cage-jarring drums that signified the approach of the King. If the music didn't move the story forward, it was quite simply cut.

The luxury of four months' rehearsal is what afforded us this way of working, and its advantages were most evident in the set and costume design. The usual procedure with set and costume design is for the actors to be shown exactly what the set will look like and what they will be wearing long before their characters have even been formed. Although the same procedure occurred with us, four months of rehearsals afforded us time for those initial ideas to be adapted to what was then created in rehearsal by the actors. For instance, I was able to ask the designer to hold back on making a certain costume for a later scene simply because I didn't feel I understood what the scene was about yet. By being able to build our characters from the foundation up, through the spoken word, we were afforded what unfortunately is a luxury in performing Shakespeare: freedom from being slave to a director or designer's take on the story, with the process rather being truly collaborative.

Sitting on the Throne

Having rehearsed the *Henry VI* plays as one long play over a period of four months makes it almost impossible to talk about the reaction of the audience to *Part I* in isolation. We performed the plays on the Swan stage at the RSC's home in Stratford, at the Power Center theatre in Michigan, USA, and finally at the Young Vic in London. The audience reaction to the productions at each venue, though different, was unanimously positive. It was also remarkable. I will never forget our first press day in Stratford. I say press 'day' because we were about to do all three plays on one day, starting at 10.30 a.m. and finishing at 10.30 p.m. I remember waking up at about 7.30 a.m. and thinking, *Twelve hours from now I will still be onstage with three more hours to go.*

At the start of *Part I* the whole cast was either onstage or dotted around the auditorium as onlookers to Henry V's funeral. As a soldier, I was standing behind the audience for this scene, which always gave me an opportunity to size up the audience. On the occasion of the press day I was horrified to see that most of the critics were sitting around the edge of the stage, fully lit and armed with notepads. The plays were staged in the round, so once onstage you couldn't escape having a scribbling critic within your gaze.

I prayed that God would get me through it, because I couldn't see how I would manage twelve hours of Shakespeare without help: forgetting my lines, cracking under the pressure or tripping on my cloak and falling over. I walked on as Henry for the first time that morning and I knew that God had answered my prayer and I would be all right. Even with this assurance I remember sitting on the throne having made my first entrance and thinking, *Will the words actually come out? Am I actually going to claim to be a Shakespearean actor in front of this audience brimming with what feels like examiners?* The words came out and I was on my way. No matter how many times we did *Part I*, the moments before speaking for the first time, having had to wait till the third act, were electric, because I could always feel this air of expectation coming off the audience It was both terrifying and exhilarating.

I had been advised not to read the reviews because of the adverse effect they might have on my performance, but my abstinence wasn't to last. I was inundated by phone calls congratulating me on the reviews. I was so relieved, not just that we had been received well but that not a single one of them mentioned the colour of my skin in relation to my performance. For me, this was the biggest compliment of all.

Part of the reason the RSC was able to undertake this massive project was the acquisition of funds and support given by the University of Michigan. As a result, we went out to perform the plays at the Power Center theatre in Michigan. It was a magical time: the overwhelmingly good audience reaction and rave reviews we had garnered in Stratford filled us with a new confidence in the quality of the shows; but nothing could have prepared us for the tidal wave of excitement and enthusiasm shown by our American audience. In Ann Arbor, Michigan, I was stopped in the street by a girl who was wearing a T-shirt with my face on it!

The Power Center is a fifteen-hundred-seat theatre, making it three times bigger than the Swan. This dramatic change called for radical alteration to the staging and very different performances from the actors. Having played the comparatively intimate space of the Swan, one of the things we lost was nuance. Little gestures and stolen moments that read on the

Swan stage got completely lost on the vast stage and in the rising auditorium of the Power Center. I was particularly uncomfortable with the size of the Power Center because, although I had played auditoriums of that size, I had never had to do it whilst playing such a substantial role. I wasn't sure how my voice would hold. Yet again that moment of having to speak those first few lines in Act III came, but this time in front of fifteen hundred people, and yet again a performance fell out of me. America was the highlight of the three venues we played; there is nothing like performing to an audience who are hungry for the play.

The joy of performing to an American audience captivated by our production of the Histories lulled us into a false sense of security. Back in London, performing at the Young Vic to three hundred jaded theatre-goers came as a real shock. We came offstage after our first night expecting thunderous applause, as was our usual American experience, only to be met with polite approval and not even a second bow. It was disheartening. To be fair, the reaction had more to do with us not yet having adapted our performance from an auditorium of fifteen hundred to a theatre one-fifth the size, and therefore blasting the audience with our grand delivery. We made the necessary adjustments and soon had them queuing round the block.

It would be difficult for me to over-emphasize the significance of *Henry VI* as a positive experience in my life. It was a learning experience that began with a phone call and continues while I write this book. Shakespeare is epic yet domestic, heightened yet humane, with universal themes that affect all humanity: love, hate, war, death, religion. The History Plays chart the lives of kings, and in three plays the life of Henry VI. It was my first major role following drama school, and as an actor I had to grow into the part professionally and artistically. The in-depth exploration of Shakespeare's themes matured and prepared me to tackle plays and parts I had once thought were outside my range.

Appendix

Any opinion of Shakespeare remains just that: an opinion, and my own thoughts on *Henry VI* are, no more no less, my opinion. This volume concentrates on the first part of the trilogy, and to keep a clear record of the sweeping events that begin here but continue through *Parts II* and *III* I've included a short scene-by-scene summary of *Part I*. I hope it provides a clear understanding and a useful reference tool complementary to my discussion of the text.

Act I, scene i
The play starts with the funeral of Henry V at Westminster Abbey. During the funeral an argument erupts between the Duke of Gloucester (uncle and now Protector of Henry VI) and the Bishop of Winchester, whom Gloucester accuses of corruption. The Duke of Bedford (Gloucester's elder brother) stops the quarrel and is in the process of restarting the funeral proceedings when a messenger arrives to announce the loss of several territories in France. The messenger blames the losses on the factional disputes taking place in England. A second messenger arrives to announce the crowning of the Dauphin as the French King Charles VII. A third announces the wounding and capture of the valiant Lord Talbot at the siege of Orleans. Winchester declares his intention to gain control over the young King.

Act I, scene ii
The victorious Charles VII and his men unsuccessfully raise a siege against the English at Orleans. The Bastard of Orleans introduces the holy maid Joan of Arc ('Joan La Pucelle'), who claims to have been divinely sent to free France. Charles challenges her to a duel in which he is overcome by Joan; she refuses to yield to any rites of love. Reignier prophesies her immortalization for heroism.

Act I, scene iii

Gloucester and his men are denied entry into the Tower of London by Winchester's men. Gloucester accuses Winchester of profiting from prostitution. Winchester appears vowing that Gloucester will answer to the Pope for his accusations. The Mayor of London defuses the argument.

Act I, scene iv

The master-gunner plans an attack on the besieging English at Orleans. Talbot, having been released through a trade of hostages, is planning an English attack, when the gunner strikes, mortally wounding Salisbury and Gargrave. A messenger announces that Joan is aiding the French.

Act I, scene v

Talbot and Joan meet and fight on the battlefield, but Joan breaks away, taunting Talbot with claims of future victories over him. Talbot tries to rally his men but fails; he reprimands them for cowardice.

Act I, scene vi

France wins Orleans back from the English. Charles proclaims Joan France's new saint.

Act II, scene i

Talbot and his men launch a successful attack on Orleans; the complacent Charles, Joan and party flee.

Act II, scene ii

Talbot, Bedford and Burgundy hold a funeral for Salisbury. They are in the middle of assessing their victory when a messenger arrives with an invitation from the Countess of Auvergne wishing to meet Talbot. He accepts the invitation.

Act II, scene iii

Talbot arrives at Auvergne's castle, only to be mocked by her. She attempts to take him prisoner, but Talbot's soldiers arrive, leaving Auvergne no choice but to entertain Talbot and his troops on their terms.

Act II, scene iv

Richard Plantagenet and the Duke of Somerset enter the Temple Garden amid a fierce argument. They go on to pick differently coloured roses to symbolize their opposition. Richard's faction, comprising the Earl of Warwick, Vernon and a lawyer, pick white roses, whilst William de la

Pole (Earl of Suffolk) joins Somerset in picking a red rose. Somerset insults Richard, citing his father's (Richard, Earl of Cambridge) traitorous ways as the reason his family lost their lands and title. Richard vows revenge on Somerset for the insult. Warwick fears the quarrel will provoke much bloodshed.

Act II, scene v
Richard visits his imprisoned uncle, Edmund Mortimer, at the Tower of London to enquire why his father was executed. Mortimer reveals that a genuine claim to the throne was the reason behind his father's murder. Mortimer tells Richard to proceed with caution and then dies. Richard vows revenge for the wrongs done against his family.

Act III, scene i
Gloucester presents his accusations against Winchester before the young King in parliament. His accusations include an assassination attempt made on him by Winchester. The King is in the middle of patching up the quarrel when the Mayor enters, announcing that Gloucester and Winchester's followers are stoning each other. The King, horrified by this, pleads for both men to shake hands in friendship. Gloucester relents in honour of the King; Winchester complies but with malicious intent. Warwick then presents a petition for lands and title to be restored to the House of York (Richard). Henry VI, prompted by Gloucester, restores them, making Richard the third Duke of York. Exeter recounts a prophecy that everything Henry V gained Henry VI would lose.

Act III, scene ii
Joan and a band of men disguised as country corn sellers gain entry into Rouen, currently held by the English. She signals by torch to Charles and his men, who then storm the gates. Talbot emerges, with Burgundy (England's French ally) and the ill Bedford. Talbot curses Joan and brands Charles and his party cowards for relying on Joan.

Talbot attacks and gains back Rouen, causing Joan and Charles to flee. Talbot then leaves for Paris to greet the newly arrived Henry.

Act III, scene iii
Just outside Rouen Joan manages to persuade Burgundy to turn against the English and support his countrymen.
Act III, scene iv

Henry meets Talbot and, for his efforts against France, makes him Earl of Shrewsbury. The King and his party exit. Vernon and Basset, respectively wearing white and red roses, begin a quarrel.

Act IV, scene i
Henry is crowned King of France. Falstaff arrives with a letter announcing Burgundy's desertion. Henry orders Talbot to march on Burgundy.

Vernon and Basset's argument continues, inciting York to throw down the gauntlet for a duel with Somerset. Henry bids them cease the quarrel lest the lack of harmony lead to the loss of France. Henry urges York and Somerset to join forces against the French. Henry also talks of the frivolity of the roses as symbols and, in making his point, wears the red rose, which greatly angers York.

Act IV, scene ii
Talbot arrives at the gates of Bordeaux but is refused entry by a French general, who tells Talbot that Charles and ten thousand men have sworn to defeat him. Talbot hears the approaching French troops.

Act IV, scene iii
York is left stranded on the plains in Gascony by Somerset's delay in despatching troops to aid him. Charles, aided by Burgundy, marches to attack Talbot at Bordeaux.

Sir William Lucy urges York to support Talbot, but York refuses, again blaming Somerset. Lucy bemoans the effects of all the factional rivalry.

Act IV, scene iv
Lucy implores Somerset to send his troops to aid Talbot. Somerset initially refuses, citing York's hunger for self-aggrandizement as the reason. He relents, but Lucy fears it will be too late.

Act IV, scene v
Near Bordeaux, Talbot is reunited with his son, whom he then tries to persuade to leave the battlefield. His attempt is unsuccessful and they agree to fight to the death side by side.

Act IV, scene vi
Talbot rescues his son and again tries to persuade him not to fight; again his son refuses.

Act IV, scene vii
Talbot laments the death of his son and then dies himself.

Charles, Joan and their party are left to gloat. Lucy asks to see Charles in order that he might reclaim the bodies of the dead. He then discovers the death of Talbot and his son. He takes their bodies claiming their deaths will birth England's victory over France.

Act V, scene i
Back at the palace in London, Gloucester announces a consensus amongst leading political figures for peace between England and France; he then cites the marriage of Henry to Margaret, daughter of the French Earl of Armagnac as a means of achieving this truce. Henry reluctantly agrees to the marriage.

Winchester arrives, having been made a cardinal. Exeter recounts the prophecy in which Henry V said Winchester's promotion to cardinal would endanger the Crown.

Act V, scene ii
Charles, Joan and their party celebrate the news of their Parisian compatriots' allegiance to the French cause. Their celebration is cut short by the announcement of the unification of the formerly fragmented English army. Joan urges Charles not to lose heart.

Act V, scene iii
Joan fears the downfall of France. She conjures up fiends, but they are no longer able to aid her.

York and Joan meet on the battlefield; he overcomes her and vows she will be burnt at the stake.

Elsewhere on the battlefield Suffolk encounters Margaret of Anjou, daughter of Reignier, King of Naples (and also niece to the French king). His attraction to her leads him to consider taking her as his mistress. He proposes that she be wife to Henry instead, which meets with both her and her father's approval. Reignier demands the French provinces of Anjou and Maine in exchange for his daughter. Suffolk consents to this, then demands a kiss from Margaret, struggling with his lust for her as he takes his leave.

Act V, scene iv
Joan is brought before York with her shepherd father, whom she denies,

saying she is of nobler birth. Her father wishes her dead. She claims to be a virgin, but on hearing that she is to be executed she claims to be pregnant, first by Alençon and then by Reignier. York and his men mock her for having claimed to be a virgin. She is burnt at the stake.

Winchester enters, announcing that the Christian states demand that peace be concluded between England and France.

York says that peace with France would nullify the efforts of the English soldiers who have laid down their lives. Warwick reassures York that peace with France will be on England's terms.

Charles and the French nobles enter to hear Winchester state the terms of peace. Charles, it is announced, will be viceroy under Henry, which Charles initially refuses, but then agrees, having been advised by Alençon that this arrangement will only be temporary.

Act V, scene v
At the palace in England, Suffolk has convinced Henry of Margaret's beauty, chasteness and eligibility as the future Queen of England. Gloucester reminds Henry that he is already committed to marrying the Earl of Armagnac's daughter, a marriage that Gloucester claims would be more advantageous both politically and financially. Suffolk dismisses this by claiming the marriage to Margaret would be just as advantageous. He wins Henry over, stating that one should marry for love and not duty.

Henry insists on marrying Margaret despite Gloucester's appeal and asks Suffolk to fetch her from France. Henry implements a tax of ten per cent of revenues to finance Margaret's arrival in England. Suffolk concludes to himself that he will rule the Queen, the King and the realm.